PLECTRUM GUITAR DUETS

Michel Héroux

I0804479

Online Audio

To access the online audio recording go to:
WWW.MELBAY.COM/31007MEB

The Taylor GT K21e and K24ce Acoustic Koa featured on the cover are courtesy of Taylor Guitars.

WWW.MELBAY.COM

Preface

Having studied both classical and jazz guitar, I have many fond memories of playing duets with my fellow students but playing duets with my teachers was an especially formative and inspiring experience. That's why I try to play as much as possible with my students now that I'm a teacher myself.

I also remember that as a guitar student, I was always asked to work on reading exercises that were very musical. This enabled discussions about playing the right notes of course, but about sound, feel, phrasing and harmony as well. It's with these elements in mind that I composed a series of short duets designed to improve sight reading on the guitar.

The duets are constructed as real little tunes, but they include a variety of difficulties, be it in rendering the rhythms or the melodies. Most of them are just straight-ahead traditional jazz duets, although some of them sound a bit more modern, and others are in the classical style. Some are easy to sight read, and others are more challenging and may need a bit of preparation.

Students: To get the most out of these duets I suggest playing them at various tempos, switching voices on repeats, analysing the harmony, and playing some lines an octave higher. You can also slide some notes or add pull-offs and hammer-ons or play some lines in octaves. Some of the duets have parts that are more like bass lines, so try playing those parts with your thumb for a smoother, bigger sound. Go ahead and experiment with the tunes!

I also strongly recommend, apart from playing in a duo with another guitarist, that you make *self duets;* record yourself playing one voice, and then play the second voice with the track you've just recorded. That's a very good way of improving your time feel, as well as your global musicianship.

Teachers: The duets can also be played in guitar ensembles, with two or three guitars playing each part. This allows the students to practice unison playing, helping them to improve their phrasing, swing feel, even-eighth feel, and overall rhythmic precision.

I hope you have as much fun playing these short duets as I had in writing them.

All the best,

Michel Héroux

To Gary

Contents

Guitars

Follow me...

Michel Héroux

medium swing

1

Guitars

Split

Michel Héroux

♩ = 120 *swing feel*

Guitars

Call & Response

Michel Héroux

♩ = 120

3

Guitars

Minor

Michel Héroux

♩ = **118** *swing feel*

4

Guitars

Blues in C

Michel Héroux

♩ = 128 *swing feel*

5

Guitars

In 3

Michel Héroux

medium swing feel

Guitars

Bounce

Michel Héroux

♩ = 128 *swing feel*

7

Guitars

Jazz Waltz

Michel Héroux

♩ = 126 *swing feel*

8

Guitars

Bossa

Michel Héroux

♩ = 126

9

Guitars

Salsa

Michel Héroux

♩ = 152

10

Guitars

Swing no. 1

Michel Héroux

♩ = 130

11

Guitars

Swing no. 2

Michel Héroux

♩ = 118

12

Guitars

Swing no. 3

Michel Héroux

♩ = 132

13

Guitars

Swing no. 4

Michel Héroux

♩ = 126

14

Guitars

Swing no. 5

Michel Héroux

♩ = 120

15

Guitars

Swing no. 6

Michel Héroux

♩ = 120

16

Guitars

Swing no. 7

Michel Héroux

♩ = 132

17

Guitars

Swing no. 8

Michel Héroux

♩ = 120

18

Guitars

Swing no. 9

Michel Héroux

♩ = 130

19

Guitars

Easy Bluesy

Michel Héroux

medium swing

20

Guitars

Swing no. 10

Michel Héroux

♩ = 126

21

17
21
25
29
33

Guitars

Saltarello

Michel Héroux

♪= 166

22

Guitars

Baroque #1

Michel Héroux

Moderato

23

Guitars

Baroque #2

Michel Héroux

♩ = 118

24

17
21
25

Guitars

Invention no. 1

Michel Héroux

♪= 138

25

13
16
19
22
25

Guitars

Invention no. 2

Michel Héroux

medium swing feel

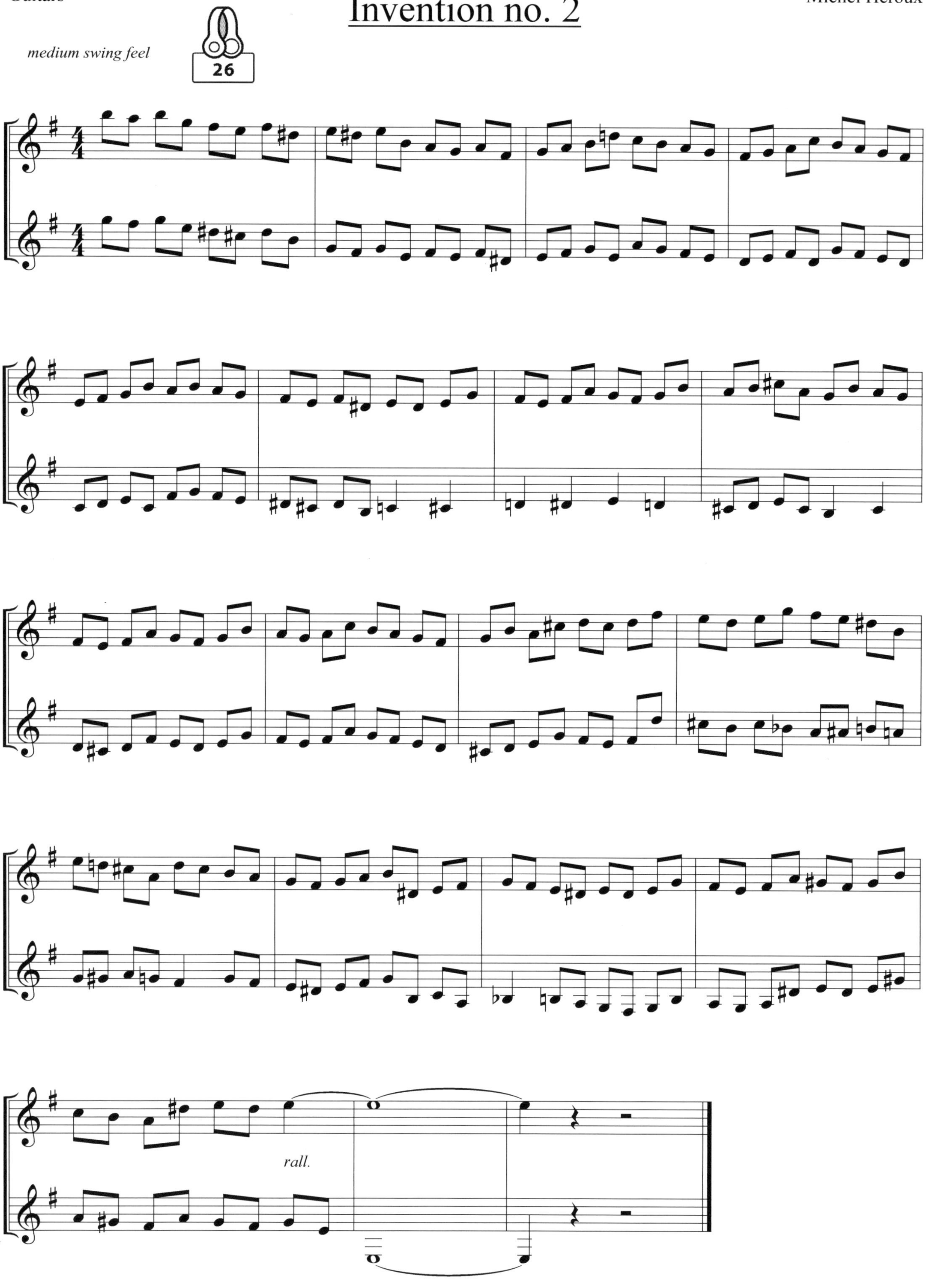

Guitars

Andante

Michel Héroux

♩ = 82

27

Guitars

Petite Berceuse

Michel Héroux

♩ = 86

28

17
21
rall.
25

Guitars

Jazz Solo 1

Michel Héroux

♩ = 132 *swing feel*

29

17
21
25
29
rall.

Guitars

Jazz Solo 2

Michel Héroux

swing feel

Guitars

Jazz Solo 3

Michel Héroux

medium swing

31

17
21
25
29

Guitars

Flea Circus

Michel Héroux

♩. = 132

32

a tempo

About the Author

Michel Héroux
Photo courtesy of Evan Shay

Michel Héroux is a Montreal-based musician/composer/educator who has worked in diverse musical environments for more than 30 years. He studied classical and jazz guitar, and later gained experience in fields as diverse as classical, jazz, rock, pop, blues, and experimental music. Michel also teaches jazz guitar at the college and university level.